SALT IN THE WOUND

The healing spirit

'Tyger! Tyger! Burning bright

In the forests of the night

What immortal hand or eye

Dare frame thy fearful symmetry' (William Blake)

Here is the last in a series of 6 books about the spiritual mind and healing spirit.

With thanks to all my dearest friends and family who have shared the journey through bipolar with me, always in my heart and the inspiration for these words of poetry.

From *'lightly coloured shadows spill over the brightening hour hands of dusk'* to "... *"In this fertile moment all petals are yellow and green the sky."*

I hope you will find something you can find alliance with and that resonates,

Enjoy the read,

Claire

This book is illustrated with watercolour paintings by the author also available as greetings cards *(boothclaire040@gmail.com)*
My dear friend, editor and fellow poetess has had the task of formatting both the poems and the artwork
Sharon Andrews, Instagram: @inksomnia_poetry

Cover design by the author Instagram: @everywordisamemory

Previous books: **Let's make tea out of roses, Roses in the tea caddy, Tea and afternoon roses, Echoes of faith and One more daisy 'til I love you.**

with overwhelming thanks to Sharon.

Contents

LAPLAND	6
BRIGHT	8
SUN BLOSSOM	10
FLY	12
SECRETS	14
SUMMER CORN	16
TRELLIS	18
THE DAFFODIL	20
AUTUMN RUSTLE	22
WINTER	24
WINTER GOLD	26
HAIKU	28
PADDED CELLS	29
IT'S NIGHT	31
TESTIMONY	33
YOUR OWN	36
BERRY RED	38
THE LAMP TREES	40
SHAKEN TREES	42
PUT DOWN THE SPADE	44
BERRY IN THE SNOW	45
THE WIND	47

POETS RISE AND FALL	49
THE FLICKER OF TIME	50
MOONLIT WALLS	52
THE NIGHT ALIGHTS	53
TODAY I CATCH A POPPY BALLOON	54
VOICE	56
DAILY VISITOR	57
WINGED EARTH	59
IN THE WINK OF YOUR EYE	61
A TWINKLE OF STARLIGHT	63
DAHLIA DREAMS	64
DREAMSCAPE	65
DEVILMENT	66
VISITING DREAMS	67
SECOND-HAND ME	68
SILVERY	69
SPRING	70
THE SNOW	71
THE FIRST WINTER	72
ROSEHIPS	74
THE FACT OF SNOW	75

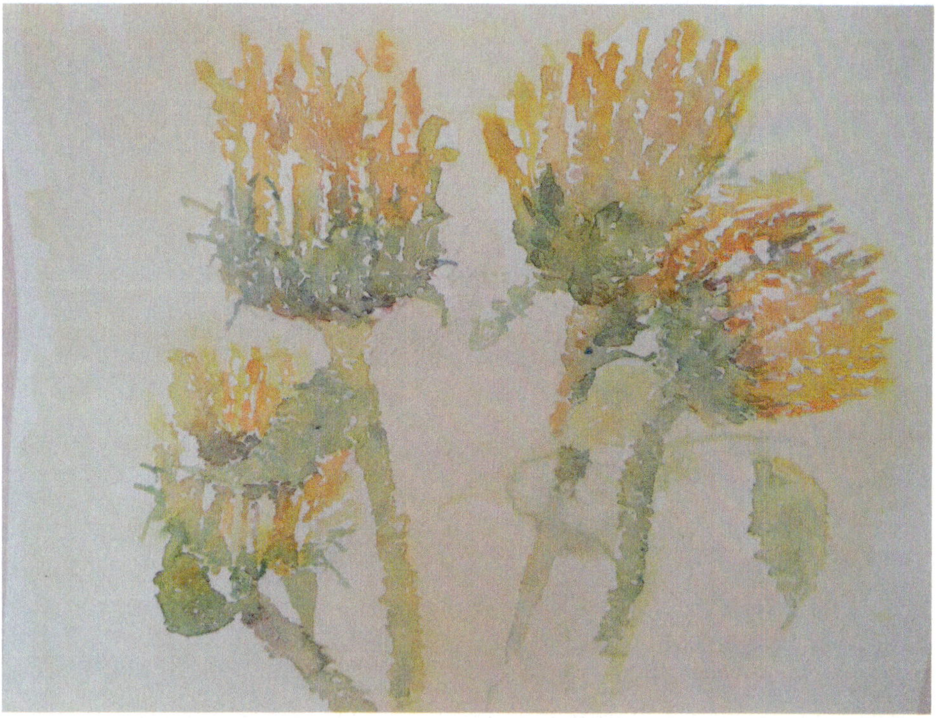

LAPLAND

You memorise the lakes,
In mists, in lisps,
Like a Christmas angel
Against my patient pillow.

Ours are the gifts,
Like the deep ploughed snow
Lingering like a recollection
Of the most glorious myth,
Shining like Christmas lights
In the winter's bare grip.

Yours are the cold lips
And freezing fingertips,
And together
We remember
A child born in December,
Turning the chill,
The bitter hearts,
To festive thrill
And to every latent miracle.

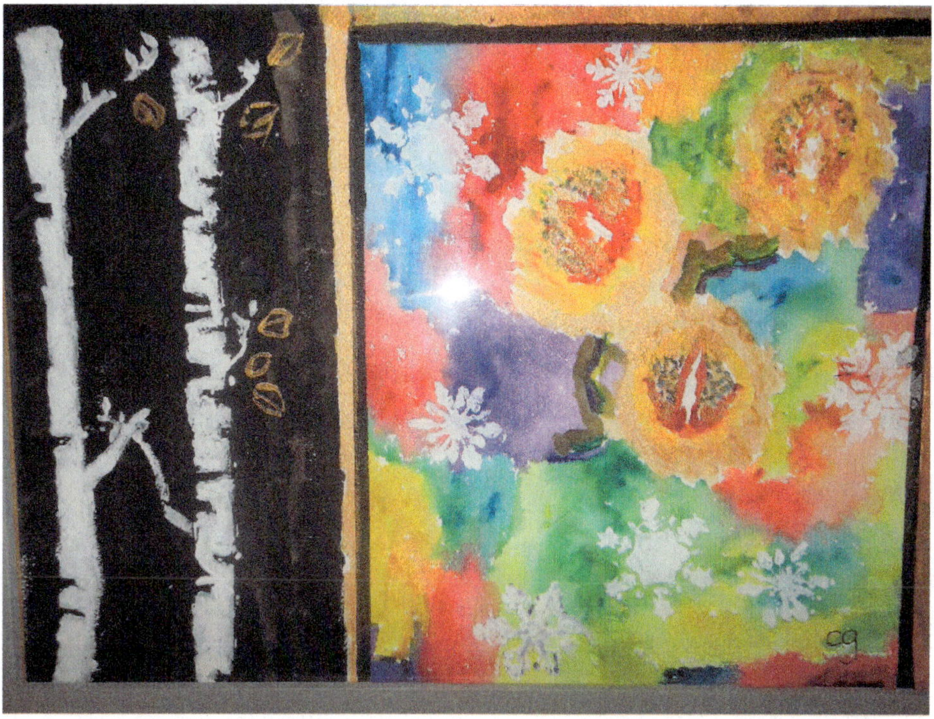
cg

BRIGHT

Bright dandelion,
Cuffed in yellow petal,
What pale loneliness leaves you so shuttered,
Your falling petals
Floating like earthbound rafts
In the darkness,
Splattering like golden shadow rasping?

Where your roots lie
The sky points in envy.
For this is where you die
And shrivel to grey.

Too slow the soil to give you up.
Too waning the rain to shower you....

....in this fertile moment
All petals are yellow
And green the sky.

And now in puffy flight
The seed is prancing
And the ghost of yellow
Seizes hold of life....

Now we are dancing.

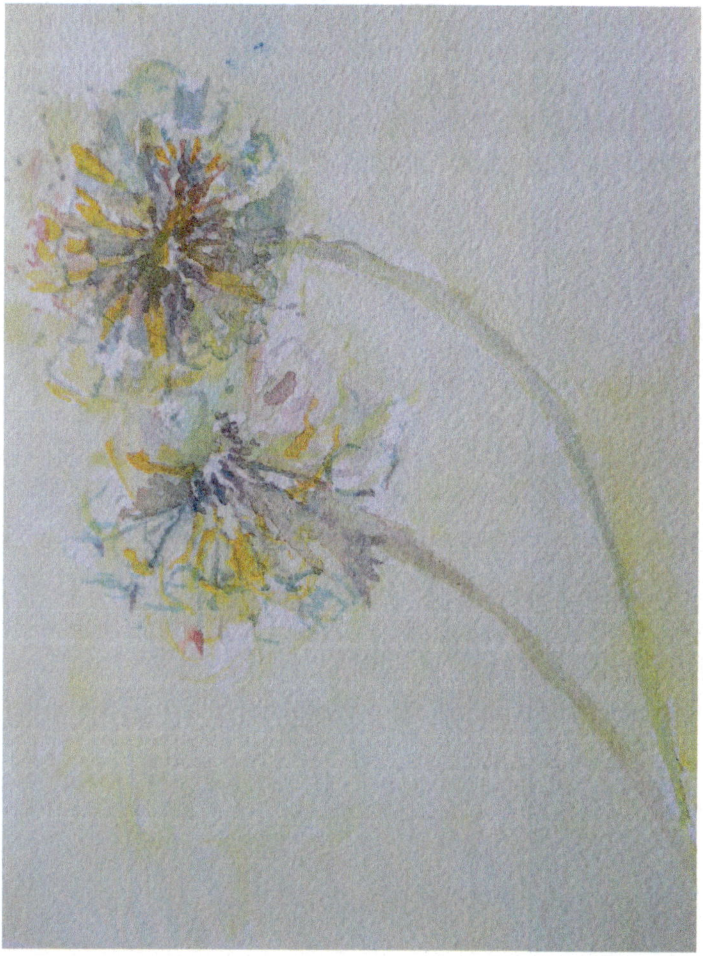

SUN BLOSSOM

He sips sun blossom
Like a mountain of golden forest
dreaming in purple.

He sips sun blossom
As it huddles in dew,
The blue light a lamp to see through.

He sips sun blossom
As the dawn crumbles fragmented
into buttermilk,

He sips blossom
in the dusk's papery film
As the evening light sips on purple nightshade.

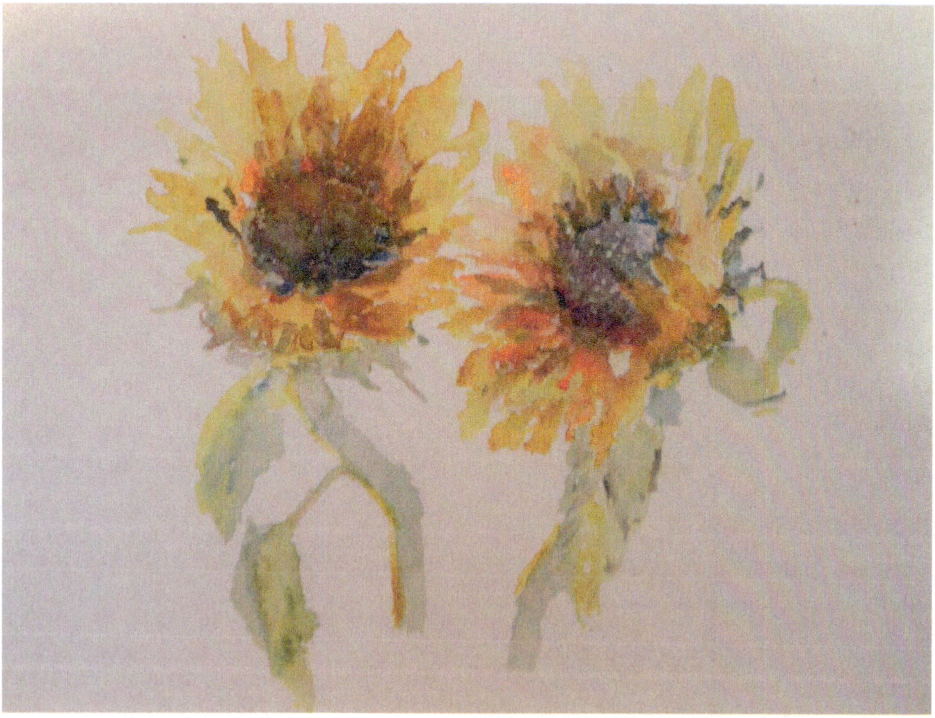

FLY

The fly's wing
Glitters like splintered glass.
She treads the air,
Pink,
Like gasoline roses.
These nude matchstick flowers
Were not real
But she knew that.

Her wings spun
Like a Catherine wheel
As if a web, unreal
Had come to steal her away.

And like stained glass
Carved in morning dew,
Vibrating
In aquarelle blue,
Winged in curvature of the sun,
She flew.

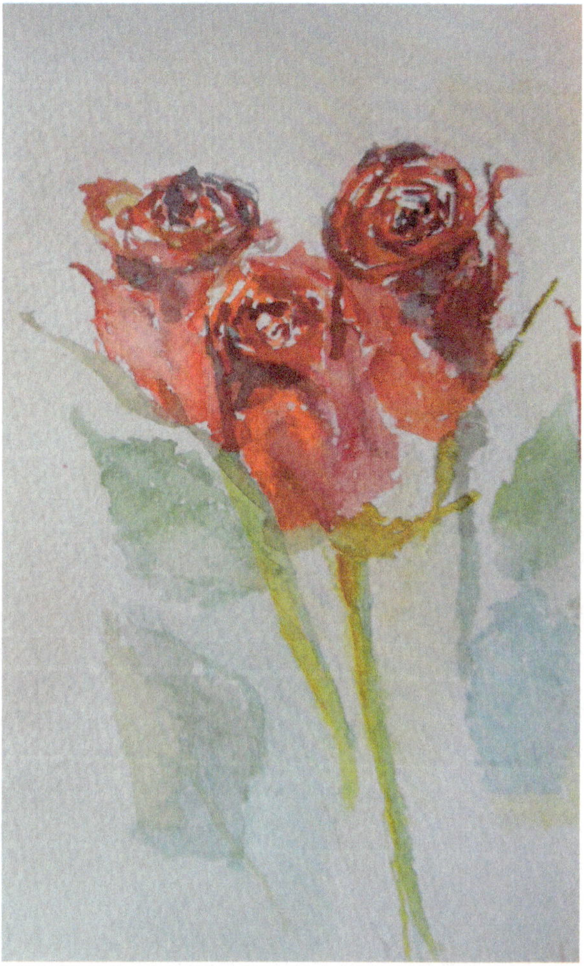

SECRETS

I am a passport photo
Validating,
The silhouette
Self-asserting.

I am the voice
Talking.
words manoeuvring.

I am the hands touching
Guarding
The gates of my garden.

I am the friend
Bursting
With joy of knowing you.

Fold back my covers
And seek me
In the madness of makeshift morals,
Seek me in the selfish anarchy
Of doubting,
the crumbling curtains
of self manufacturing.

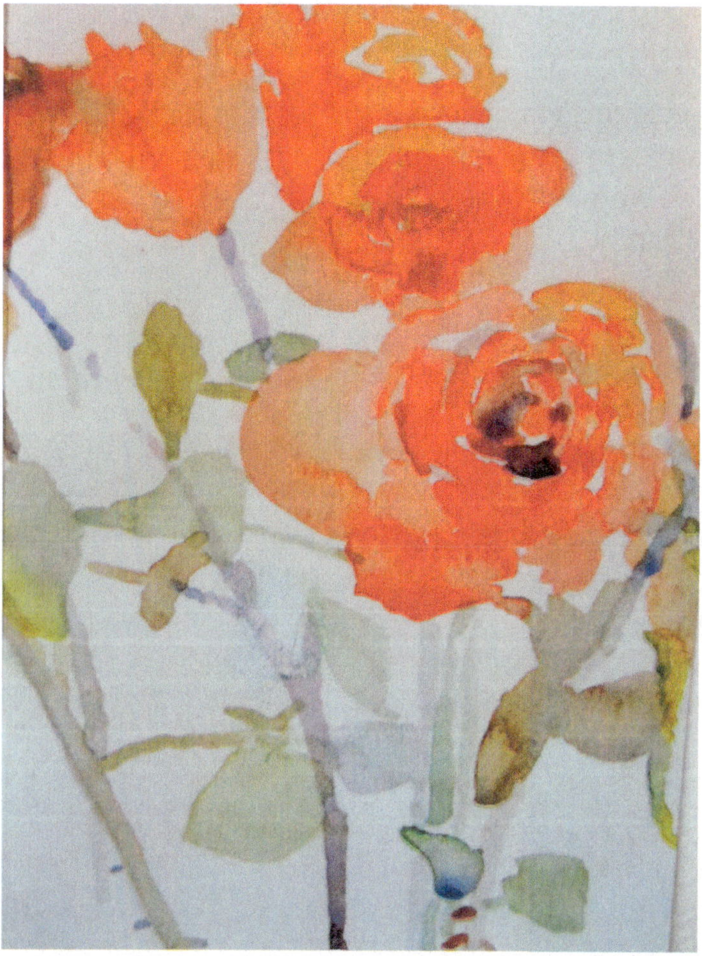

SUMMER CORN

High the golden crest of corn
Like a warbler in the glassy sun,
Throat tied with this butter wand
All to gaze upon.

High are the winds
That sweep your willowy ends
To the cages of the sky,
The golden crest of corn flies by.

High the fields that shift,
Dizzy,
Rumbling in green,

High the golden crest of corn,
Giddy,

And then as you are trampled upon
At harvest time,
Blend with the rueful earth.

Make it summertime.

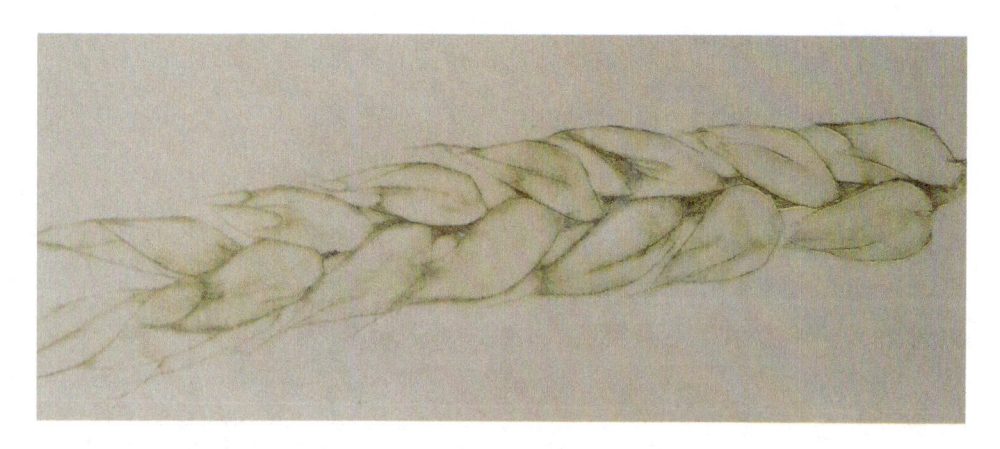

Josephine Gibson, artist and print maker

TRELLIS

Like a trellis
The treetop shook.
A network of leaf,
Filtering the lacey wind
Like a glugging brook,
Stroking the calypso of light
Like a golden tambourine.

And when the storm stopped
There was only a bluish vein,
Leaves clicking like castanets,
No sign of pain,
Colour filled again.
And above all,
The air,
Swirling warm and cool,
Suggested a song,
Between puffs,
Splashed with joyful rain.

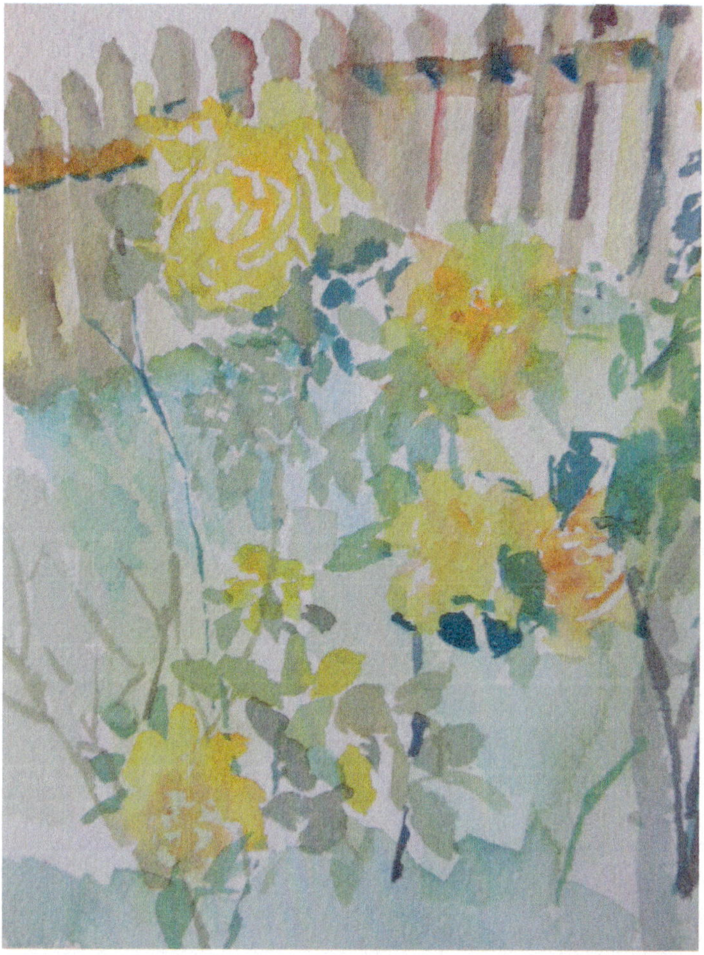

THE DAFFODIL

The daffodil glows happily,
Beautiful
In the memory of snow.
And summer ripens autumn
In the tabby leaves
That she blessed
When her blue skies ceased.

But winter grieves
In a startling chill
For she knows not
That spring will come
And again the daffodil.

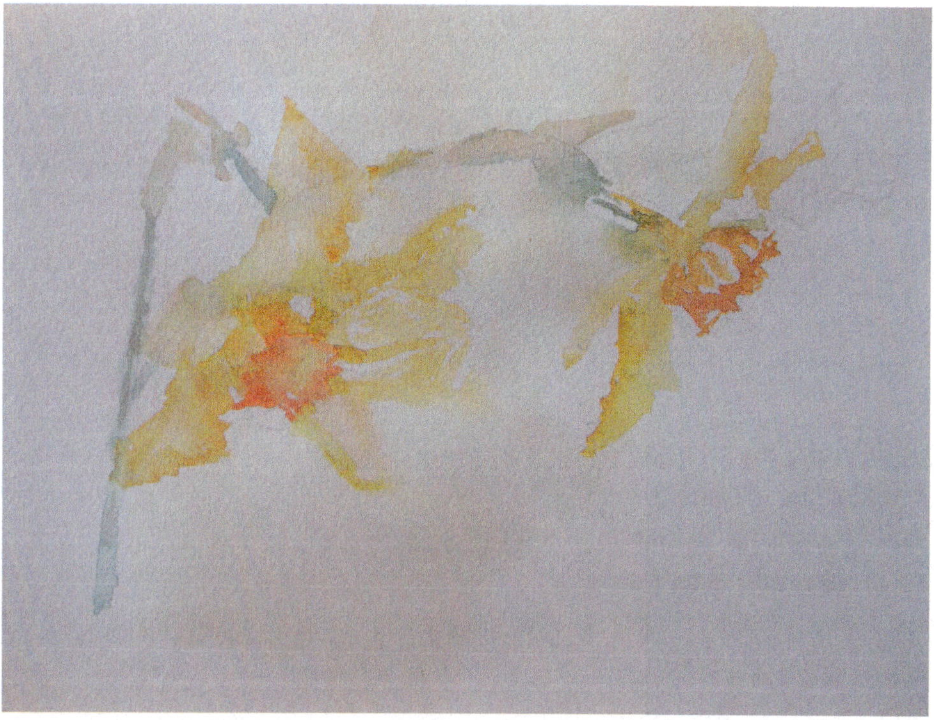

AUTUMN RUSTLE

There is a small movement
In the autumn leaves.
I bite back the tears
For love is here amongst the trees,
Amongst the leafy fringe,
Through greyness and nothingness.

I bite back my tears
For love has found again
The chestnut autumn
As if she had never gone,
As if she had never blown away.

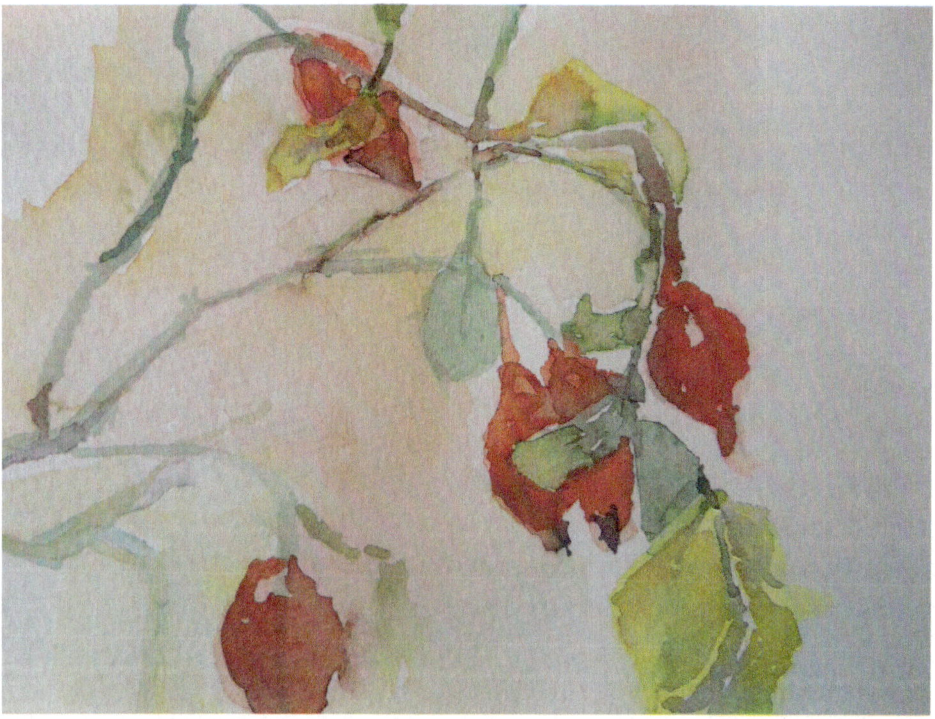

WINTER

Winter,
Along her cold walls of snow,
Sped.

Light separates
In sparkling strands
Undoing a snowflake's web.

 Quietly wrapped in gloomy grief
The lagging sound of grieving …
… on Winter's withered, whitened earth,
The snowdrops each adorning.

So while the skirts
Of frilly chill
Around the branches hang,
Sweet winter shawl
We pardon you
For bringing us your sting.

Keeping close your warm intent
To hurry along the Spring.

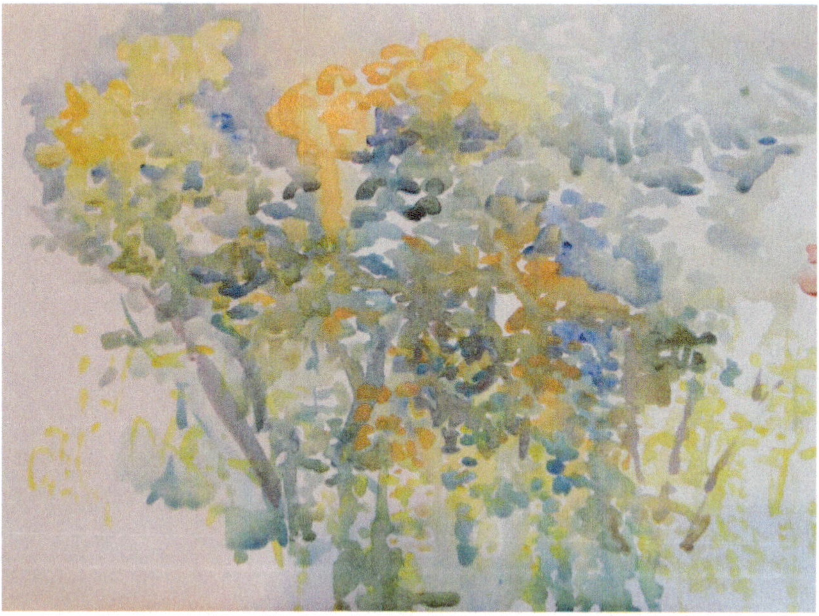

WINTER GOLD

Under the dome of sky,
Trees, bones of gold
Rhyme with the earth
And hoary Winter.

She pulls the blade
From Winter's spectre
To re-set the shoots of green
To claim the secrets deep within
To claim her secrets deep within.

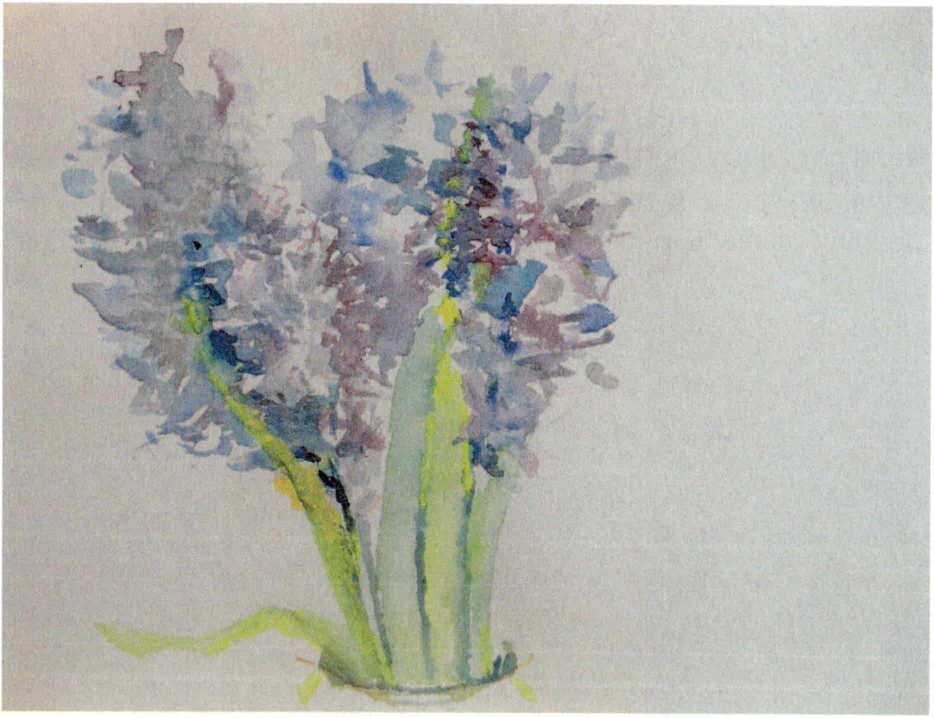

HAIKU

The night winds shuffle
Between the dull waking and
Sleeping of shadow.

PADDED CELLS

The hallway blushed
With puckered rooms

The red, the smell,
Of polished wood,
Like a judge's court.

Where are the marks,
Left on these cushioned,
Keyless doors?

The mind's lung breathed,
Blushed
And the hallway hushed
In moonlit psalms,

Better read them.

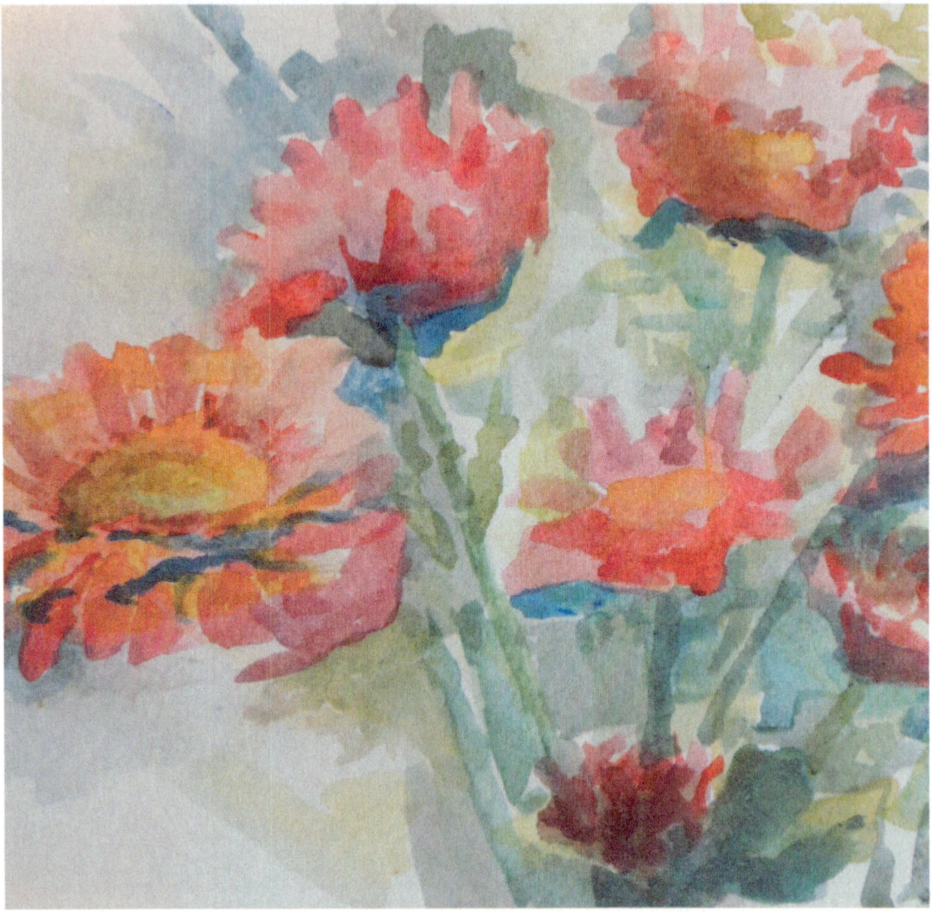

IT'S NIGHT

It's dark
And it is Night.

It's still Night,
How about that.

Weary,
Putting right
the twist and turn
of the lively day
where is my nightly vial
The curtains of grey?

Put out the gaslight,
her violet flame,
let the Night
Close her lids
close, close
her lids again

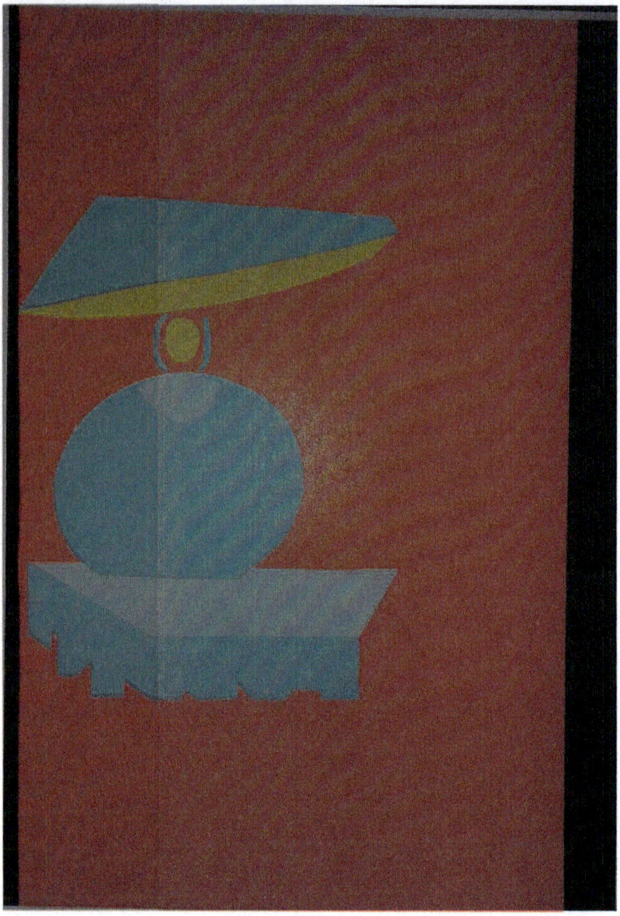

TESTIMONY

Inward,
Horses and roses,
Cottages bright
In the twilights of her mind
Break the inner tears
Like reminiscent particles
Of herself.

Strange pipes of thwarted melodies
Call beauty to rise and fall
In ghostly mourning.

A melancholic feather
Flew the distance.

The spine trembles
Is it the gold in your plume
That traps the tangerine wind?

Rising to jasmine,
Split plumage,
Never to be herself again
Until the waves of joy draw back
Along the woven track.

Is it the gold in your plume
Or is it the moon
That sinks inwards and outwards,
That traps the tangerine wind?

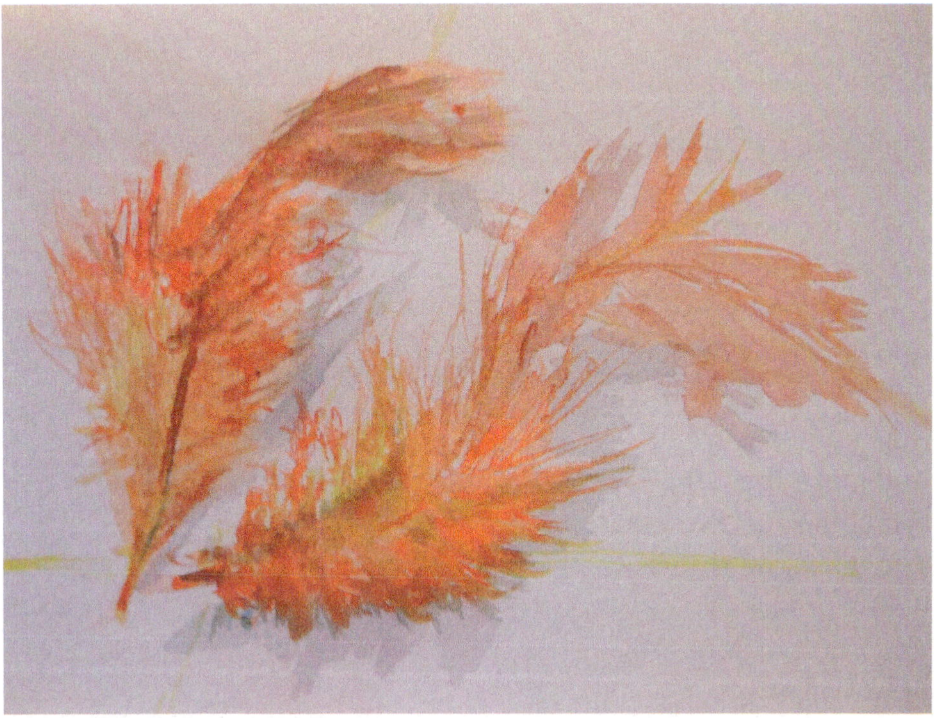

YOUR OWN

Hold your own hand
Wipe the gritty sweat from your palm
Speak your own truth
Protect yourself from harm
Love your own ways
And how they resound.

Hug your own dreams
And make them big
Worship your own ideas
And make them stick
Be the preacher
And listen to your prayers
Above all this
Set the world alight
With your cares.

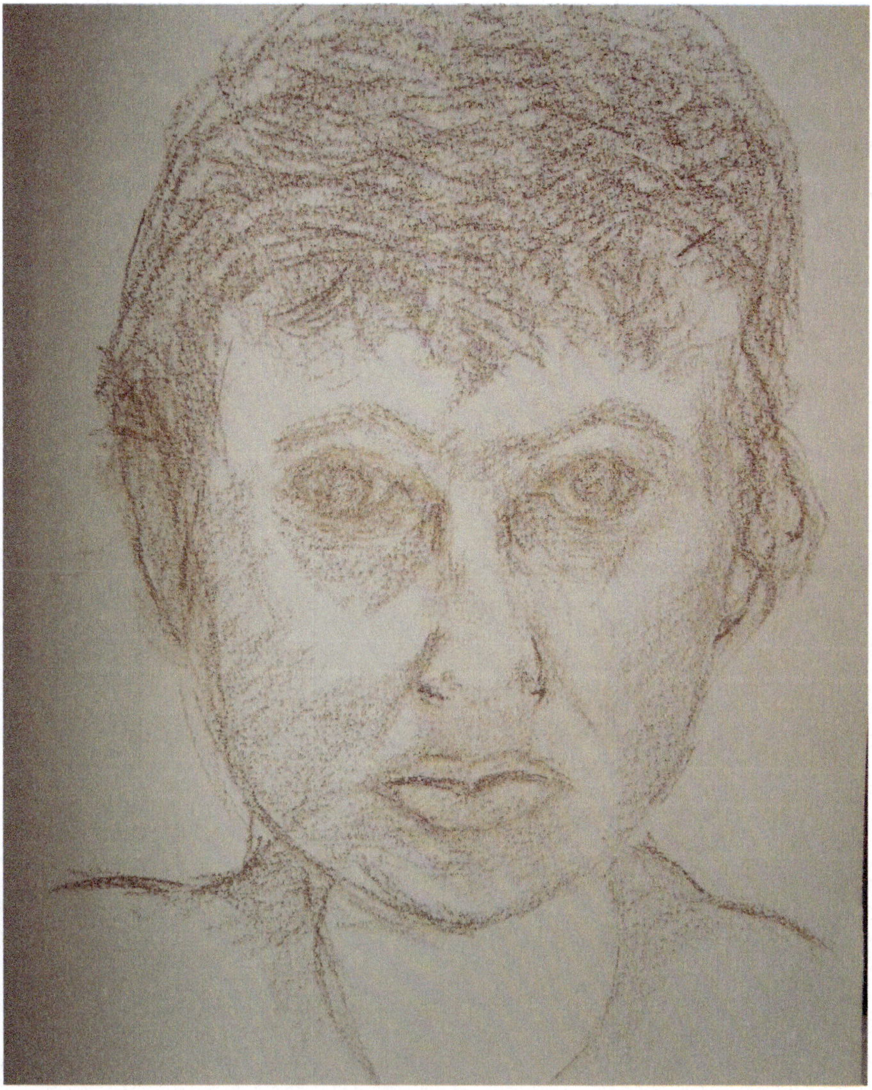

BERRY RED

If each berry were wine
Trees would be in red gowns,
Sunk to the ground,
As if buried in berries.
Snowdrops, against Robin-red
Could not cool the blizzard of tears
That we shed,
The tears, berry-red,
Spilling through the curls of the cherry,
Tinsel-red,
Like the wine of our sorrow,
Berry-red.

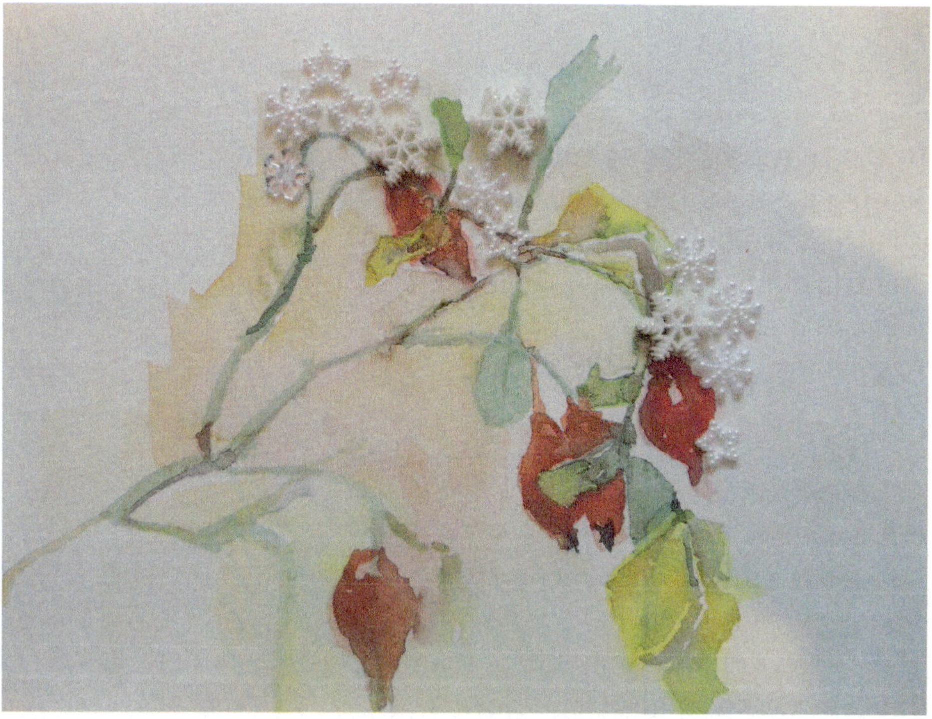

THE LAMP TREES

As the light goes gently out
Marooning the lamp once bright
The trees like bubbled matchsticks
Stand like sentries,
A line of poesy
Against the serrated sky.

Old lamps,
Cerise with embers glowing
Put down their heads,
To lay the light still flowing,
No longer showing
The earthly clouds around them roaming,
The grey dark umber of light slowing
Falling under the earth's crust foaming
Whence fertile seeds were shyly growing.

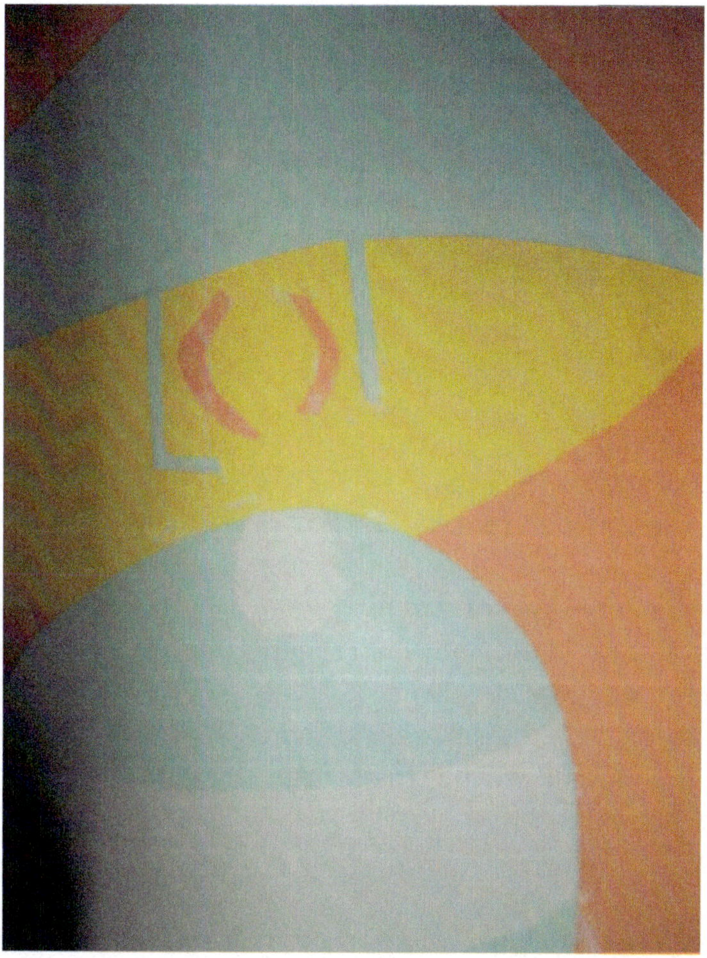

SHAKEN TREES

Shaken trees
Display their brightest leaf
When blossom
Salutes the sky in grief.
The pearly veins,
Like silvery maps,
Show, like lanterns,
The steely road,
The road of steel
Winding like a golden reel.

'Tis true the fiery blaze of green
Stood upright for love to be clearly seen.
'Tis true the way was clearly lit,
And blossoms, dimpled stirred and shook.
'Tis true the moon knew not the route
But shot the path,
With bow and arrow,
A silken hope
For a sweet tomorrow.
A joyful love to end all sorrow.

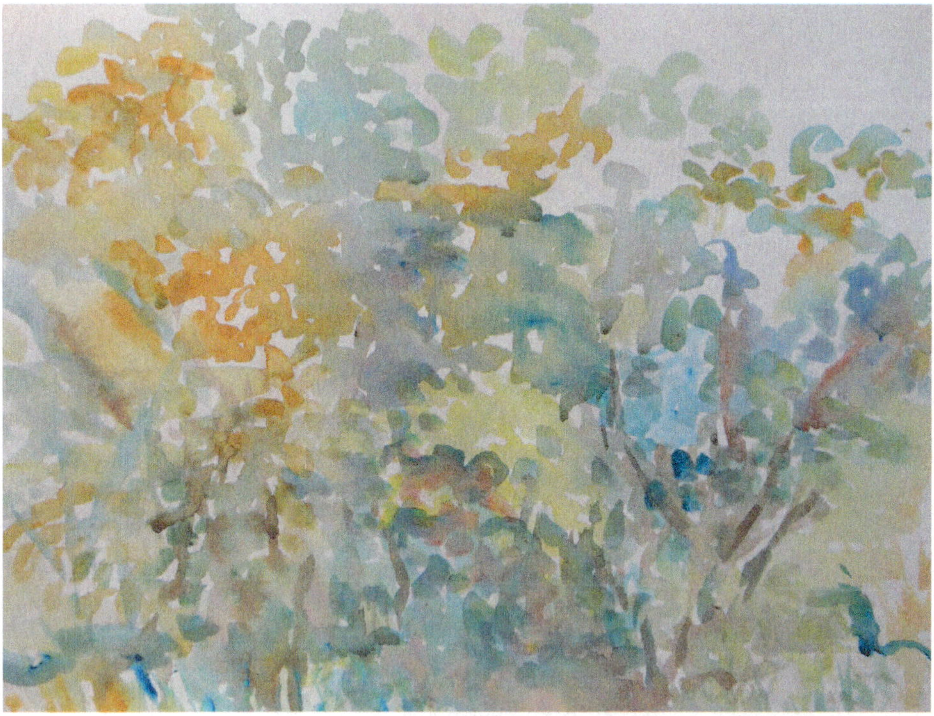

PUT DOWN THE SPADE

Put down the spade
The garden is dug.
Lift now your brow
The seed is sown.
Let out a breath
The sunshine is shining.
Go to the door
For newness is brimming.

BERRY IN THE SNOW

A berry loses itself
In the snow.
She glistens
Thistle-purple
Under dabs of white
Little head swept
In the windy starlight.
Such a rotund fruit
A feast for the winter bird
Lost to the crisp cold
A sorry and a deadly plight.

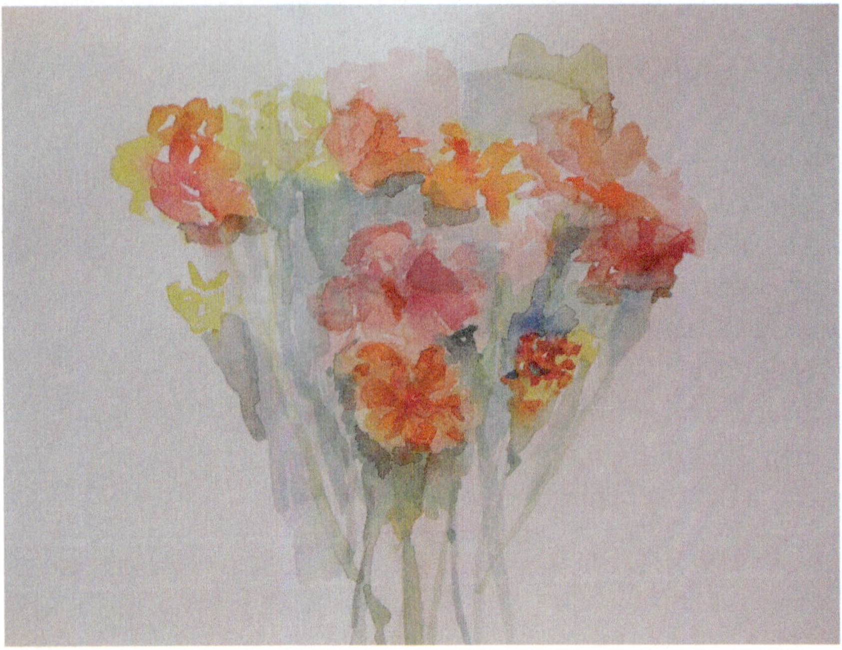

THE WIND

I ran away in the early hour
From the coloured tower
Asking me to wait.
For in the singing turrets
The wind called out your name.

What heed I paid
Hid the purple clouds
Of my longing,
The purple clouds
Of my longing

So the tower
Stopped to watch my valour
The wind she stopped me in my tracks
In my tracks she stopped me.

And as the wind turned me sharp
And clouds pale blue did blow
The tower spelled your name so bright that I could not forget
The way the coloured turrets sung
My love,
The day I was bereft.

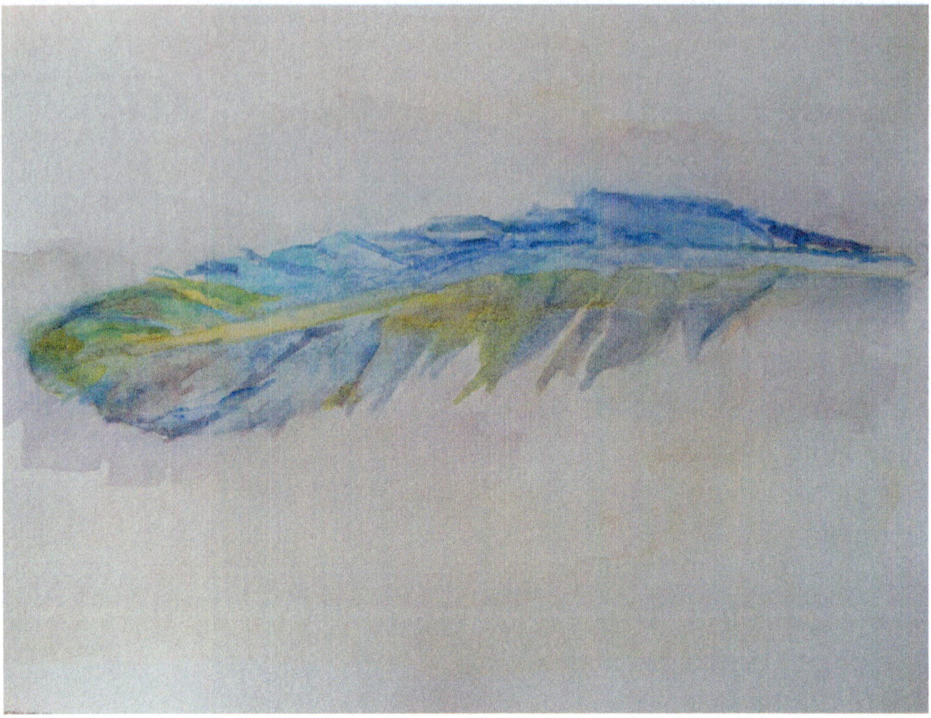

POETS RISE AND FALL

Poets rise and fall
Along hushed poppy walls,
A dash of red shadow,
Various against the red umber earth.

The lands of drifting sanguine
Make bitter verse,
But there lie our memories,
Dull and terse.

Poppy fields we will remember,
Your deeds we always spurn
For in each burning flower
A heart is gravely torn.

Away the red,
Away the hurt,
Splashed in the dusty dirt,
As the poets rise and fall
Along the poppy wall.

THE FLICKER OF TIME

Between a clock
And its interfacing
Lies a fixed world,
Mushroom cottages
Stand there
As if in tin villages.

Dripping through the tears of time
A beautiful bell
Lay with its interfacing
Soft against a ghost face
Cushioned and still.

What clock winds back
Its wizened hands
To set the time again

And the sun switches to the moon
Like a counter
Flicked ticking across the room.

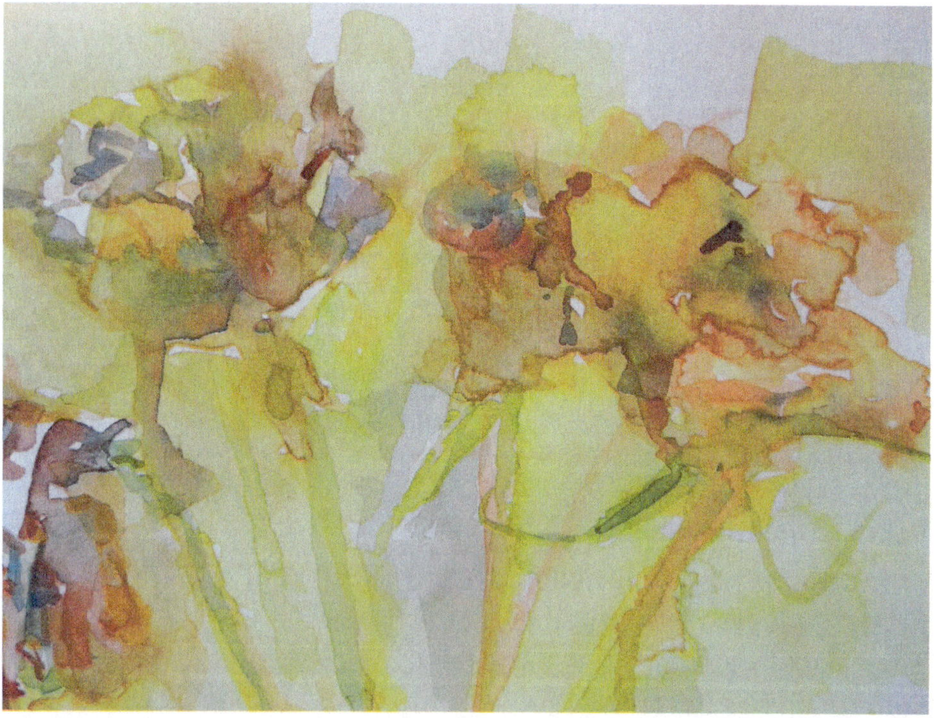

MOONLIT WALLS

The light is apricot.
Like tinsel through the window
It scratches the moonlit walls.

Bright shadowy fingers like spindles
Beat, tentacled in orange.

The angel shadows
Thicken like lilac straw
Passing the moonlit walls

Crunched leaves dim under
The drunken stars.
Something has passed.

Tinsel falls from the moonlit walls.

THE NIGHT ALIGHTS

A winter night pierces the fragile dullness
Of snowy earth.
Brilliant in blue her soft mauve shadow
Makes fierce pools around icicles
As light unfastens herself from glittery ice,
Folding like shells into the dark...
The dark that tingles through holes
In yellow snow,
And holds the leaves above the frost-
Frozen moments of bitter loss....
The night that blows her gentle gloss
Like thrushes' egg in ample glare
For angels and the glistening air...
And how the Night had cast her spell
That owl could tuck under her wing
The snowy woods, the shadow jewels
And everything left suffering.

TODAY I CATCH A POPPY BALLOON

Balloons, like the notations of Spring,
Blown like coloured flame,
Pass the wind,
And the trees,
The sky.

Heaven knows why
Balloons make a song
Across the wind,
And the trees,
The sky.

Wondering and dreaming
They rise like rubies,
Bursting in a dash
They fall in glossy pools,
Full of miracles.
Today I catch a poppy balloon.

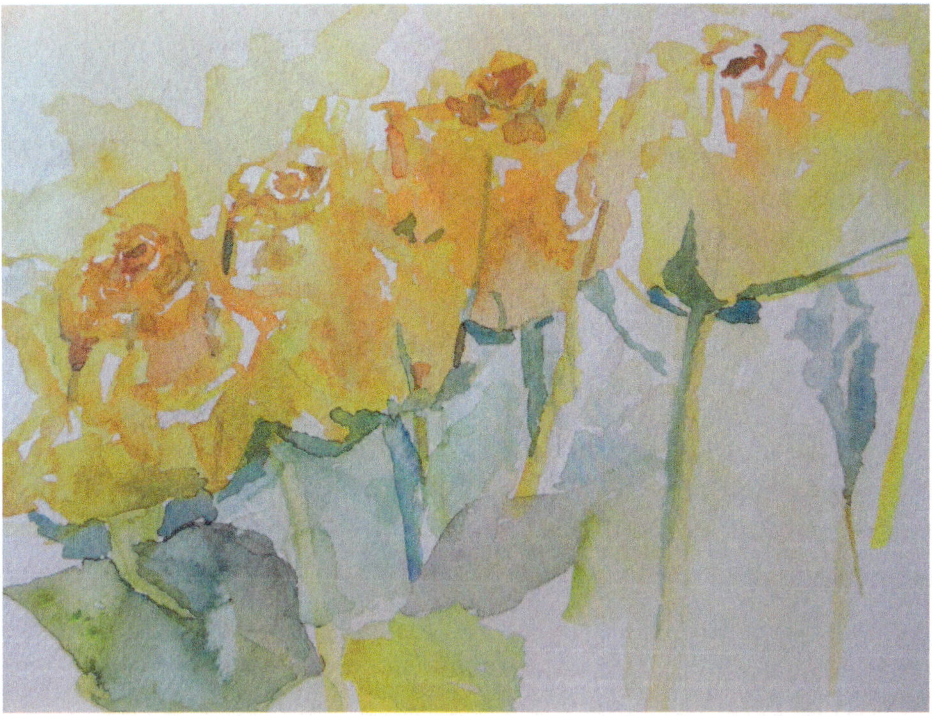

VOICE

My voice is thinning,
The trees lose their colour,
Splatter, splutter,
Blotting the paper,
Monsters colour my words,
Splatter, splutter,
My voice is withering
The ink of my voice has dried,
Blotting the paper
I sob with no pulse,
No pulse to cry.

DAILY VISITOR

Find her on the windowsill
Masked against the pip of daylight
Birds flap by
You'll find her there,
You'll find her on the windowsill
Pulling the earthy Night
Into the lamplight.
She sits still,
Eyeing the rotating fishbowl.
There is not much going on today.
much as usual.

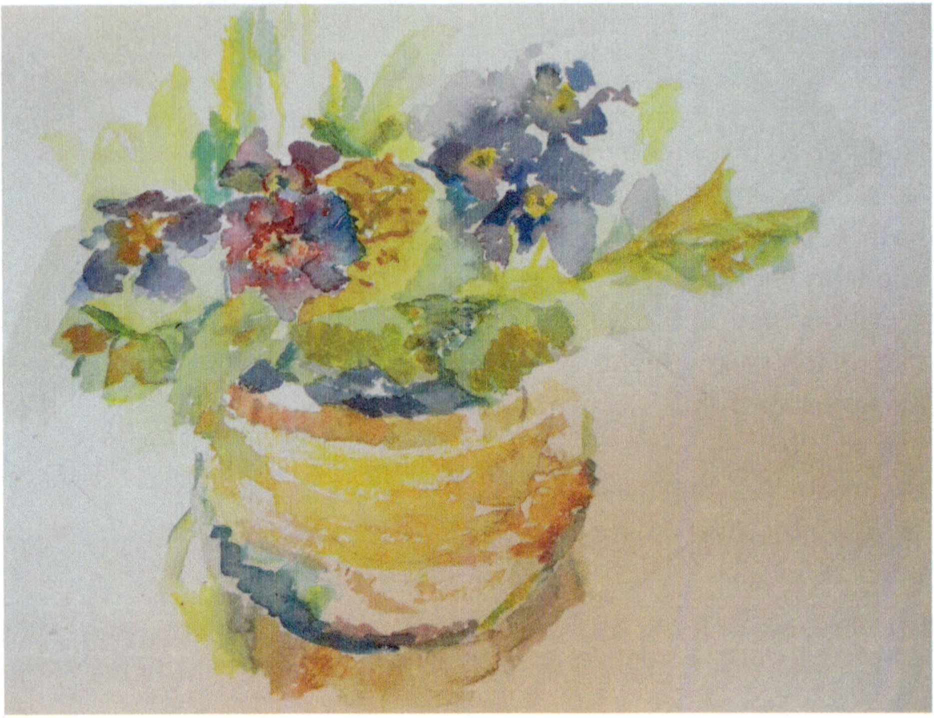

WINGED EARTH

The earth displays a lilac –blue complexion
Winged like a dragonfly
In the water's reflection,
Ziggy wings
Gather like a silky mantilla-
Little rings of gold,
Bells of music
Around her to unfold.
The earth is yellow,
Dribbled in salty light.
Golden moths
Her darkness to ignite
Where love fills and fulfils.

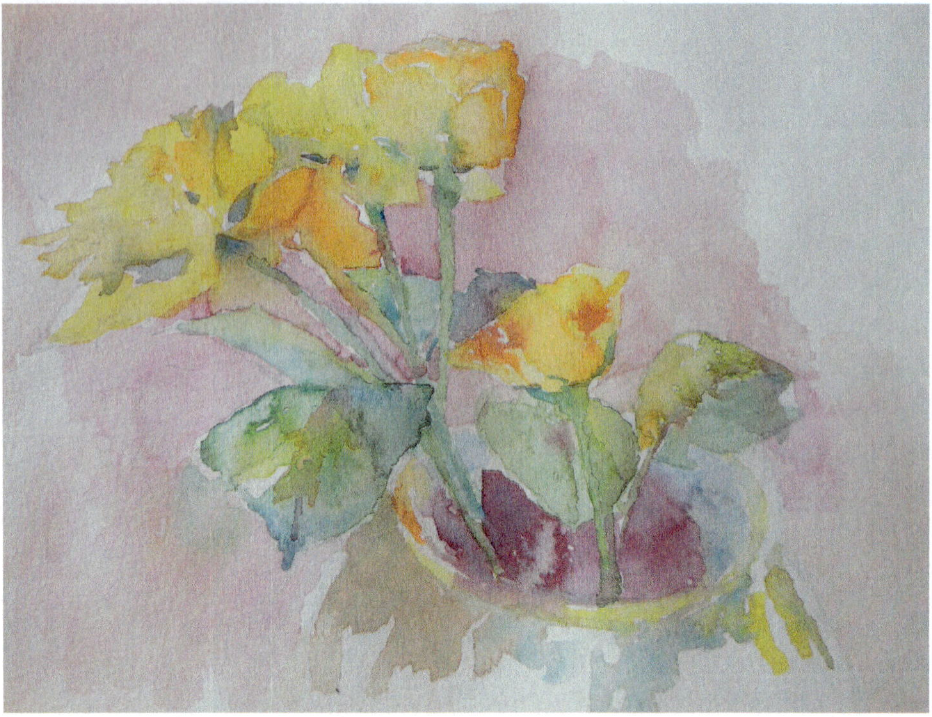

IN THE WINK OF YOUR EYE

In the wink of your eye
You tell me
It will be ok.

With a touch of your hand
You tell me
The sun will rise again.

In a pretty voice
You tell me
All will be well.

And in the warmth of your smile
I am told
Yes everything will be ok.

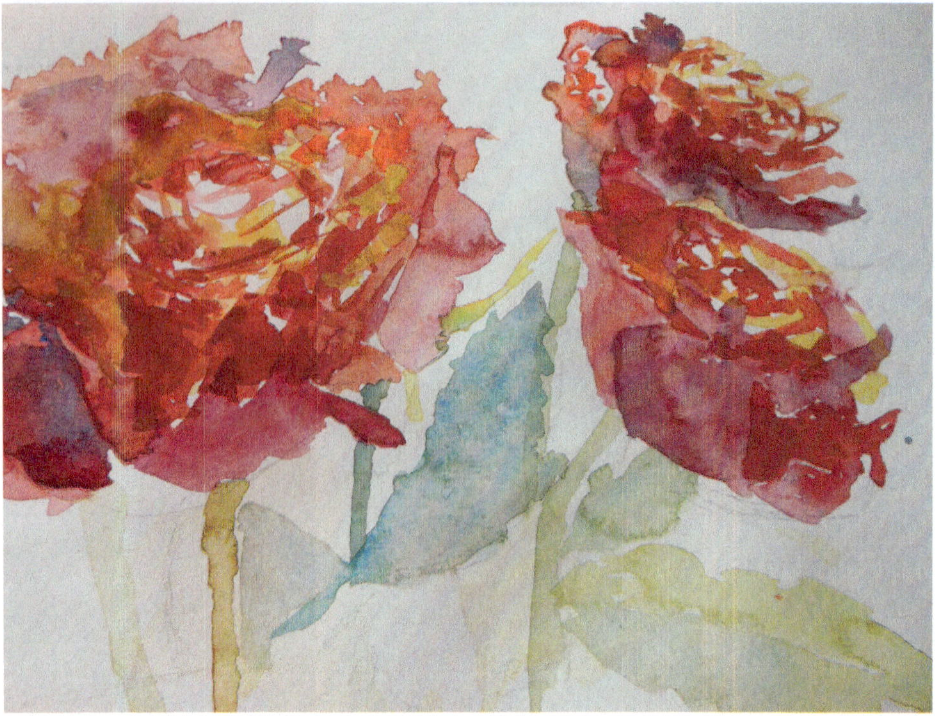

A TWINKLE OF STARLIGHT

A twinkle of starlight
sheds willowy tears
into the Night.

You are silver
I am gold
He is the canopy of wise.

Grey flakes turn to stars
It is snowing now
I am told.

DAHLIA DREAMS

The gentle ridge of dahlias
Stumbles over cut grass,
The sigh of sun swelled,
Grazing softly
Lightly coloured shadows,
Spill over the brightening
Hour hands of dusk,
Their golden heads,
Ringed with petals
Like the seconds of a clock.

Will Summer dedicate herself
To Autumn,
Winter to Spring
Without mentioning the peal
Of ticking dahlias
In the mosaic
Of a colourful dream.

DREAMSCAPE

Let's dream our way through life,
Her swirls maroon and gentle white,
Let's dream.

Let's dream through the heavy drones of Summer,
Watch her curly roses as they ramble
Let's dream.

Let's dream about frisky clouds,
Mirrors of lakes through the dirty old towns,
Let's dream.

And let's dream loudly
About the swelling gold mountains,
The emerald twinkle of trees,
Let's dream loud through the zebra rain,
The sting of cold on our windowpane,
Through the slippery Nights,
The lightening that strikes,
Let's dream hard,
Let's dream.

DEVILMENT

Let the devil give you a fright,
That's right,
Pull you through the sky
By your wrist,
Fly, fly,
Like a witch way up high!
Twinkle your cuff link, clink, clink,
Take a cocktail drink, don't think,
Forget the starry night
The universe is out of sight.
Take a drink, go on, don't think,
Go for it, you are on the brink,
The witch with the flashy broomstick.
Let the devil give you a fright,
That's right,
Take the wind between your teeth and ride,
Feel the shiver,
Feel the thrill,
See the spoils of the devil's will.

VISITING DREAMS

My dreams awoke
Where shadows met
Like fingers, grey,
As thirsty masts
Round the lapels
Of windless sails.

I catch my dreams
In a dusty net
On a sleepless night
That never slept.

Fingerprints like veils of gold
Awoke my dreams where shadows met.
Fingertips like suns uncoiled
Woke my dreams
To the Night that kept
Her dreams in shadows,
Ash and ink,
Half sleeping shadow of a fingerprint.

SECOND-HAND ME

Hand-me-downs,
Winter jumpers
Are oh so twee
And uh so dreary for me.

Don't you see
Your second-hand junk
Was never meant for me,
So damn dull,
I want to be free.

Even your mirror doesn't look like me
Can't you see
Your second-hand clothes
Make me feel unreal
Don't you see
This is not a second-hand deal.

SILVERY

Silver fruit of the tree
I felt plucked by thee,
Don't you see,
Washed away in tumbling silver,
Silver.

SPRING

The wick's flame is full
With yellow daffodil,
And we are needful things.
Where is our path straight and narrow,
Pointed like spring arrows?
Where are the buds opening
Across the tattered grass.
Where are the lively happenings
Of April drifting past,
Let the winter find a track
To carry the wilting snow.
Where is our path straight and narrow?
For all seasons the wind does blow,
Let us follow bud after bud
Until her flower is all we know,
Leaving winter's trickle just enough
Against the cold to make us glow.

THE SNOW

Why does the snowdrop still sing
When the light around her
leaves nothing to brighten
Her suffering?
How does a whitened bud
Keep growing
When it keeps snowing?
When the ground is solid,
From frost?
Too harsh the season
Too cold the wind
For such a gentle flower
Blown in snowy showers.
Why does she still sing
In a winter dark and dim?

THE FIRST WINTER

Snowballs of golden white
Softly land on porcelain paths
Where flecks of airy light
Are flicked by snowy slurry
Up into sparks like shot silk.

Upon the road
Captive silent songs
Stir winter trees
As if the dancing snow
Could breathe, voice her intent,
Crisp among chilly leaves.
Mole-like, the winter month shelters,
And, lighter, full of flurry
She spreads her icicles like dull
Luminosity
And snowflakes tingle
Like the muffled pat of symbols
On her frosty nose.

Winter has not forsaken
The tinted earth
Where snowy flames lie
Sparkling on virgin soil.
For this is Winter's birth.
She is not forlorn at all.

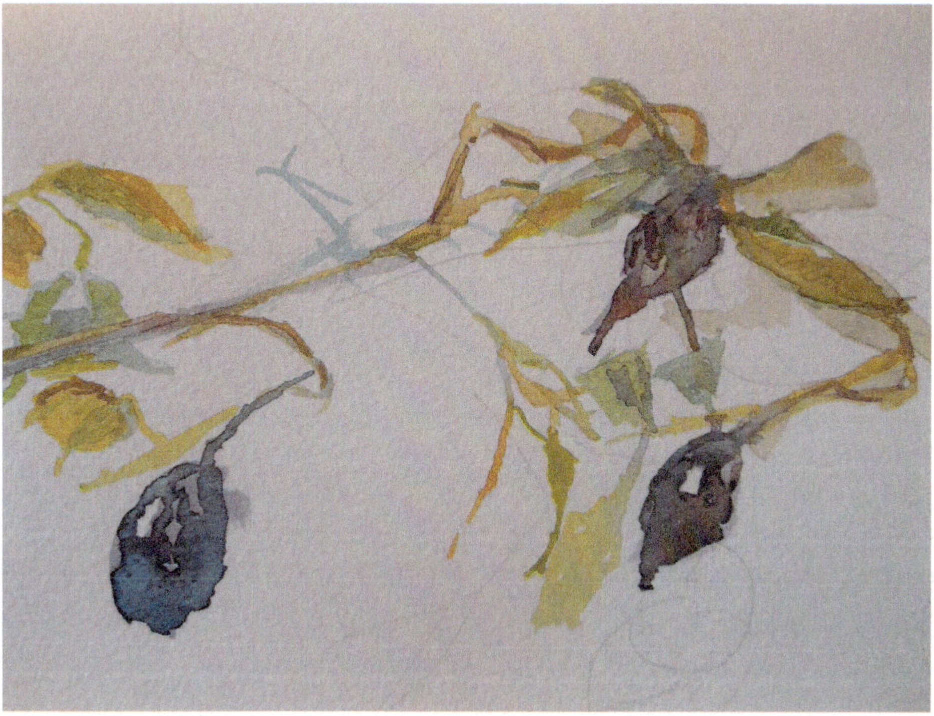

ROSEHIPS

Rosehips had never been
So full and sumptuous,
Bursting bright and beautiful
In sun-filled frost,
Purple and golden.

The berry clouds startle the snow.
Through each snowflake
They must glow,
Damson and dimpled,
Small and wintry
In hoary winds of glory
They are blown.

THE FACT OF SNOW

The fact of snow and her crystal flakes
The way the wind breaks
Into a flurry of white,
Snow skating in a sky of grey light.

The fact of snow and her thud
In handfuls of cuffed scoops of delight
The fact of snow picking up grit
In between children's fingertips.

The fact of snow sliding down windowpanes
Snowing pitter patter like rain
On the hard earth
Telling of the patterns she makes
On leaves crisply lying beneath.

The fact of snow
Cold against the heart of the dear,
Beating in hurried clusters
Bearing only her bright fleece
At this time of year.

The fact of snow.

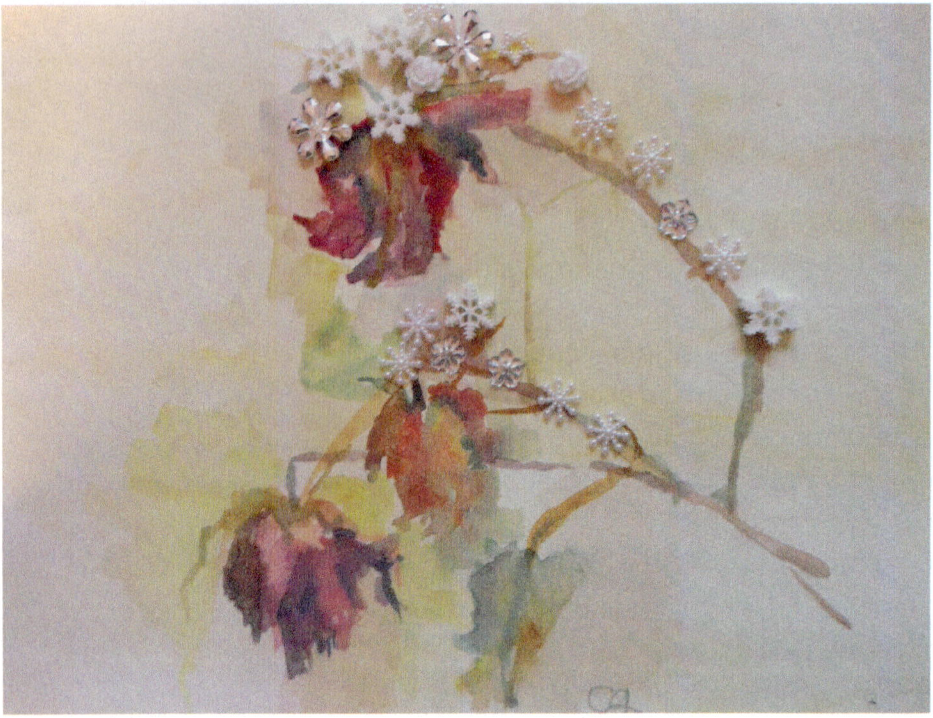

Printed in Great Britain
by Amazon